Nami Says

Written by Iman Europe
Artwork by Amanda Kaufman

Nami Says
Copyright © 2018 by Iman Europe.

All rights reserved. No part of this book may be reproduced or transmitted in any form or by any means without written permission from the author except in the case of brief quotations in articles or reviews.

Cover illustration by Amanda Kaufman.
Layout and design by Iman Europe.

Published by Good Soil Productions.
ISBN: 978-0692188026

First Edition: 2018
Printed in United States of America.

to my God who molds me,
my mother who knows me,
and my father that grows me,
this is all because of you.

to the lovers who couldn't feed me,
the friends that didn't leave me,
my family that needs me,
this is all because of you.

to the women who inspire me,
the men that admire me,
the children who aspire to be,
this is all because of you.

now i am the wiser me.
more fight, more drive, more light in me.
i've finally found the higher me.
and it is all because of you.

thank you.

foreword
by **malanda jean-claude**

i first heard 'nami' in earthquakes before ink became devotion. i had never told anyone about my first heartbreak. a balled fist trapped in a sandbox and emotions too hard on the air. i was only a boy when i discovered water. shards mistaken for ballads & roses for eyelids until you touched them— clean. 'do not dive head first.' you forget your own wingspan when they untwist your first knot. truth is expandable when eroding with pain. at the mouth you find blood is synonymous to a river, beauty returns in shards but at least you have a mirror. before this. no one has ever mistaken your skin for rain, you will be mistaken for air. the ground will move at your pulse. and after losing yourself, you will come to one simple truth: it is inhuman to not live in your own heart. the pain you log into memory is only ammunition for a greater freedom. nami is your wingspan. your baptism into bone— into remembrance;

when truth no longer chokes and shards
become water. here, you will find the gravity
inside of your home.

introduction

i remember realizing that i wasn't who i wanted to be. i had given away so many pieces of myself that i became unrecognizable to me. all that remained was a soul of scraps, an exhausted heart and a neediness to change. i was a caterpillar. disconnected and discontent with my own reflection.

but something told me that there was untapped power waiting inside me. when i looked past the present, i saw the evolved version of myself— healed and healthy, strong and wealthy, appreciated and undefeated. i made the decision then to find that design.

in metamorphosis, they call this self-made decision "molting". this is when the juvenile hormone leaves the caterpillar and it begins to begin again. the caterpillar cracks open its original skeleton and crawls out of it, then creates a new skeleton from the inside of itself. i find this process fascinating, because nature insists that we must break out of our old selves before we become who we are meant to be.

i'm convinced that our lives are split amongst three phases: the caterpillar (where we begin), the chrysalis (where we evolve), and the butterfly (where we become). i also believe that everyone's process is different, and some will spend more time in one phase than others will. still, i believe that we are all meant to continuously transform.

i wrote this book as an aid to every phase. not because i am a prophet, but because i am a human being who has grown and is still growing. the way to waste a life is to become complacent with it, and although evolving isn't the easiest process, it is indeed the most fulfilling. george carlin said, "the caterpillar does all the work, but the butterfly gets all the publicity," so understand that all the effort we put into bettering ourselves will bear fruit in the end.

i sectioned this book into two parts. the first is *Nami Says*, a book of my sayings, proverbs and imanisms. these are things that i've learned throughout my journey that i hope will encourage you along yours. the second part is *I Say*, a book of affirmations to speak to your inner butterfly. these are high frequency thoughts, that, if believed and practiced, will come into fruition.

keep reading and find what speaks to you.

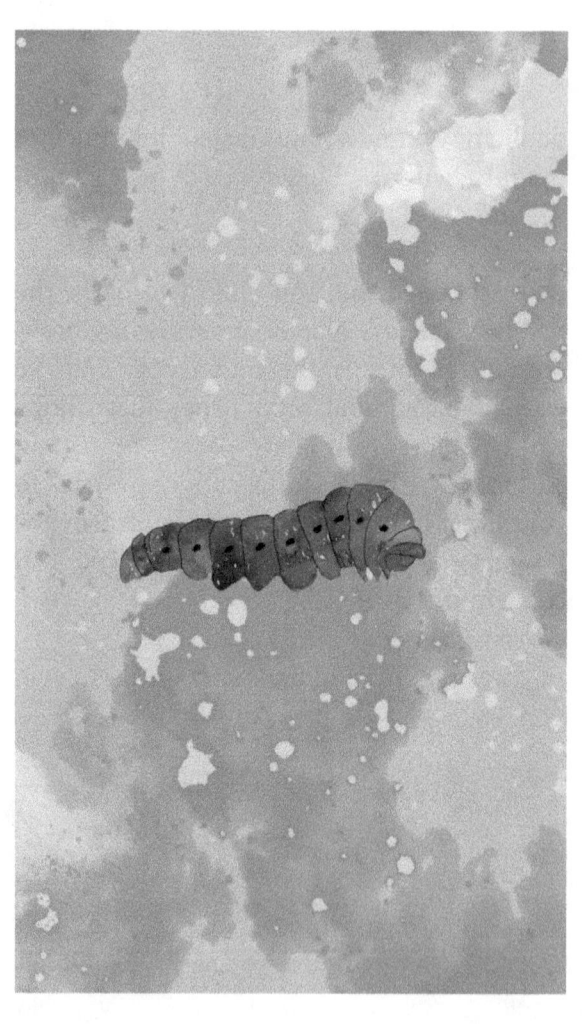

PART ONE:
Nami Says

Nami Says:

if you want it, grow for it.

Iman Europe 1

Nami Says:

the bridge between
thought and accomplishment
is focus.

Iman Europe 2

Nami Says:

spend your energy wisely.

Iman Europe 3

Nami Says:

be the kind of friend that you need;
to others, but also to yourself.
replace self-criticism with patience
and allow yourself room to grow.

Iman Europe 4

Nami Says:

choose self-preservation over exhaustion.
peace over conflict. growth over comfort.
faith over worry. and honesty, always.

Iman Europe

Nami Says:

> what's beyond you
> is greater than
> what's behind you.

Iman Europe 6

Nami Says:

you are supposed to be
exactly where you are right now.
your present position
is a part of your process.
you have an important purpose,
so it will take time to prepare.
be patient. you will arrive on time.

Iman Europe 7

Nami Says:

it is better to be prepared for an opportunity
and not have one, than to have an opportunity
and not be prepared.

Iman Europe 8

Nami Says:

as you elevate, it will seem lonely.
familiarity will become distant, your values
will change, and the only constant will be
yourself. keep rising anyway. space is being
made for you at higher levels.

Iman Europe 9

Nami Says:

restructure is just as important as structure.

Iman Europe

Nami Says:

we all have two things:
talent and time.
one is an unlimited resource, one isn't.
use your time wisely.

Iman Europe 11

Nami Says:

stop expecting honesty from people
that lie to themselves.

Iman Europe 12

Nami Says:

see yourself right.
recognize your worth and your
potential, your growth and your light.
you are prepared and you belong in high
places. you are blessed and you are beautiful.

Iman Europe 13

Nami Says:

allow yourself to fall in love with yourself.
piece by piece.
over and over.
time and time again.

Iman Europe 14

Nami Says:

the purest love is love without expectation.

Iman Europe 15

Nami Says:

sometimes plans fail.
not because *you've* failed,
but to give you a new perspective on
how to succeed.

Iman Europe 16

Nami Says:

every situation has an advantage
and a disadvantage.

Iman Europe 17

Nami Says:

healing requires balance and forward
movement. feel, but don't dwell. reflect,
but accept. protect yourself, but keep your
love warm.

Iman Europe 18

Nami Says:

everyone can't handle the love that they say they want. most aren't ready and don't realize it until they get it. don't let that discourage you. keep your love the same. but this time, redirect it back to self, and then to someone who is ready to know, ready to grow, and willing to try.

Iman Europe 19

Nami Says:

trust is a choice. trust is a grace.
trust is giving vulnerable pieces of yourself to
someone else. trust is vital to the growth of
any relationship. trust is the foundation of any
long-lasting partnership. trust is a gift
that is earned; only to be given
to those who are worthy of it.
but trust is an inside job.

Iman Europe 20

Nami Says:

plot twist:
everything you are waiting on
is waiting on you.

Iman Europe 21

Nami Says:

healing doesn't always mean
digging deeper and dissecting yourself.
sometimes, it simply means
letting things go and letting things be.

Iman Europe 22

Nami Says:

remember your resilience.
you are made of elastic, not glass.
everything that has tried to break you has
failed, repeatedly. your strength is worthy
of recognition.

Iman Europe 23

Nami Says:

be emotionally responsible.
don't love when you are not ready.
don't toy with emotions out of insecurity.
don't be anywhere your attention isn't.

Iman Europe 24

Nami Says:

karma will always make sure
that you feel the same feeling
that you've been sending.

Iman Europe 25

Nami Says:

the only way through it... is through it.
shortcuts and escapism will only
delay your healing. it is better to
face the pain now and feel it in full
than to live a life weighted by baggage.

Iman Europe 26

Nami Says:

be the loyalty you wish to experience.

Iman Europe 27

Nami Says:

the only person you can save is yourself.

Iman Europe 28

Nami Says:

true freedom is in forgiveness.

Iman Europe 29

Nami Says:

if you have nothing good to say, say nothing.

Iman Europe 30

Nami Says:

the best thing to do
is usually
the hardest thing to do.

Iman Europe 31

Nami Says:

some will want you to belittle yourself
for the sake of their comfort.
obeying them would be foolish.
head high, spirits high, expectations high.
always.

Iman Europe 32

Nami Says:

keep your focus forward.
the quickest way to stumble
is to run while looking backwards.

Iman Europe 33

Nami Says:

why are you rushing if you aren't ready yet?

Iman Europe 34

Nami Says:

why are you asking for more if you haven't
taken advantage of what you already have?
eat what's on your plate.

Iman Europe 35

Nami Says:

we live in cycles—
of joy and pain,
sun and rain,
loss and gain.
when you find yourself back in the valley,
remember that the peak is just a cycle away.

Iman Europe 36

Nami Says:

love yourself through it.

Iman Europe 37

Nami Says:

find gratitude in the midst of it all.
favor finds those that are thankful for what they
already have. you have more than enough.
find ways to be productive with it.

Nami Says:

what if it's all a part of the plan?
what if you need to build *this* strength
and learn *these* lessons
for the next phase?
and what if *this* phase
is the prerequisite
for your evolution?

Iman Europe 39

Nami Says:

God never shows His hand.

Iman Europe 40

Nami Says:

at any point in time, you can redirect your
energy. at any point in time, you can change
your mind. and most times, it's just that shift
in perspective that can change your life.

Iman Europe 41

Nami Says:

beware of spiritual warfare.
there are forces that don't want you to win.
there are forces that don't want you to live.
there are people that are on assignment
to distract you from yours.

Iman Europe 42

Nami Says:

have the faith of a child
and the courage of a lion.

Basil King said, "be bold—
and mighty forces will come to your aid."

Nami Says:

mind-traps that immobilize you:
doubt.
worry.
pride.
hate.

all stemming from one emotion:
fear.

Iman Europe 44

Nami Says:

feel the fear and go anyway.

Nami Says:

some parts of life you'll go through alone.
some things people won't understand
and some things you won't explain.
learn to be your own comfort,
confidant and confirmation.

Iman Europe 46

Nami Says:

the beautiful thing about this life is that it's only yours; tailored only to you. no one else can experience it from your eyes, read it from your mind, feel your pain or fully understand your process. so live for you, love for you, experience for you, and make this life what you believe it should be.

Iman Europe 47

Nami Says:

growth happens in isolation,
but depression does too.
remember to come up for air.

Iman Europe 48

Nami Says:

suicide is a permanent solution
to a temporary problem.

Iman Europe

Nami Says:

don't become a prisoner of your own mind.
get out of your head, get out of your way,
and live to experience.

Iman Europe 50

Nami Says:

self-love and selfishness
are not synonymous.

Iman Europe 51

Nami Says:

when you find love—
don't let your mind get in the way of your heart.
don't force it. don't try to recreate yourself to
fit into the expectations of what you <u>assume</u> that
person wants you to be. be genuine, be direct,
be transparent, be you.

honor that love with persistence,
commitment, loyalty, trust, service, safety
and communication.

Iman Europe 52

Nami Says:

when you give love—
give it as an offering, not a loan.
learn to love in freedom, not in bondage.
they deserve room to grow and space to
experience apart from you.

find balance in the love you extend
and the love you preserve for yourself.

Iman Europe 53

Nami Says:

be thankful for those who
reveal the parts of you
that still need growth,
and love you through it.
iron sharpens iron.
this is true friendship.

Iman Europe 54

Nami Says:

no experience is ever lost.
as long as you're living,
every experience will come full circle.

Iman Europe 55

Nami Says:

make sure:
your words match your actions.
good intentions aren't good enough.

Iman Europe

Nami Says:

your life is bigger than you.

Iman Europe 57

Nami Says:

don't give too much too soon.
reserve your energy. limit your access.

Iman Europe 58

Nami Says:

compare yourself only to your former self,
not to someone else's path or purpose.
everyone has different measurements
of success, different advantages and
disadvantages. focus on *your* life.
that is the only way to enhance it.

Iman Europe 59

Nami Says:

listen to your spirit.
there are truths that only
intuition can tell you.
follow your heart.
it's your personal compass
and it knows what it needs.
quiet your mind.
it's fickle and it lies sometimes.

Iman Europe 60

Nami Says:

there is a difference between
wanting someone to evolve with you
and wanting someone to change for you.

Iman Europe 61

Nami Says:

measure a man by the way he handles difficult situations. does he acknowledge or does he ignore? does he apologize or does he avoid? are his actions aligned with his words? there is an unmistakable difference between a man and a manchild.

Iman Europe 62

Nami Says:

choose the healthier option.

Iman Europe 63

Nami Says:

make your mountains small.

Iman Europe 64

Nami Says:

everything works together.
your past is in alignment with your present,
your present is in alignment with your future,
your failures will be the reason for your success,
your hurt will be the cause of your healing, and
your tests will become your testimonies.
keep going. everything is working
together for your greater good.

Iman Europe 65

often times, it's our own thought patterns that limit us. we spend so much time and energy questioning our capabilities, but in the midst of doing so, we diminish our own power. i remember when yiri, my lifelong friend and manager at the time, encouraged me to run a crowdfunding campaign to help fund the start of my music career. i shunned the idea— not because it was a bad one, but because i didn't believe i had enough support to successfully pull it off. two years later, with more courage and a healthier perspective, i took a leap of faith and ran a kickstarter campaign. not only did i succeed at raising $10,000 to fund my first album, but the contributions from the campaign allowed me to self-publish and distribute my first book, too (the one you're reading right now)! i had so much support from friends, fans, family and strangers and the love was overwhelming. i could never thank them enough for the love that they showed me.

in that experience, i realized that the universe responds to conviction. when you are firm on what you want and you declare what you believe, the law of attraction will create that reality for you. this is why affirmations are so important. they are positive proclamations of who you truly are. they speak of the butterfly version of us; our full and future selves. it wasn't until recently that i realized how powerful they were, and because they have worked so well in my life, i wanted to create a few for you to practice as well. feel free to tear them out and tape them to your mirror or wall for morning rejuvenators, or simply leave them here, whichever works best. just try it out. find an affirmation that resonates with you, read it daily, meditate on it, and pay attention to how it changes your life.

when a caterpillar evolves into a butterfly, not only does its physical form change, but its mind does too. in fact, while transforming in its chrysalis, it develops a brand new brain. and as we evolve with a shift in perspective, healthier thoughts and higher expectations, i believe that we can do the same.

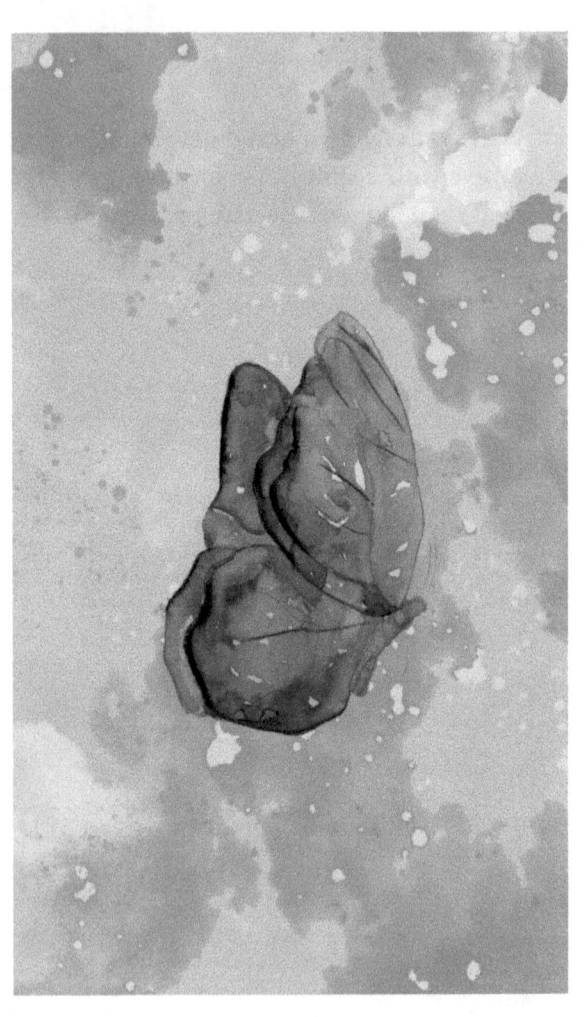

PART TWO:

I Say

I say:

(write your own)

I say:

I will give no circumstance
more power than my own ability.

Iman Europe 68

I say:

I will be the best version of myself today.
I will be committed to my future goals.
I will think long-term.
I will be better than I've been before.

Iman Europe 69

I say:

I am not worried about anything outside
of my control. It will all work out for my good.

Iman Europe 70

I say:

I am financially responsible.
I spend consciously. I save for the future.
I make the most out of what I have.
I am grateful for what I have.
and because of my gratitude
and financial discipline,
I will continue to increase,
and continue to find new ways
to be wiser with what I am given.

Iman Europe 71

I say:

I am strong in mind.
I am strong in body.
I am strong in sprit.

Iman Europe 72

I say:

I am far more beautiful than I am flawed.
I will speak more of my beauty
than my flaws.

Iman Europe 73

I say:

I am worthy.
I am unstoppable.
I am able.
I am adequate.
I am smart.
I am stable.
I have everything that I need.

Iman Europe 74

I say:

I trust my process.
I trust God's timing.

Iman Europe 75

I say:

I am digesting and releasing toxins simultaneously.
I am healed, yet healing.
I've grown, yet I am still growing.
I thank God for His blessings.
I thank Him for His blockings.
I have faith in the bigger picture.
I am learning to choose myself first.

Iman Europe 76

I say:

I will not be discouraged.
I will not be shaken or swindled by fear.
I will be like a tree; strong and free.
firm in who I am, firm in my beliefs.
I will not allow present problems to rob me
of my prosperous future.
I will trust my vision and see it through.
I will not be discouraged.

Iman Europe 77

I say:

I will make the best of my day,
because it was given to me.
because there are people that I have lost
that no longer have life as an opportunity.
they remind me of the blessing of breath.
they remind me to be the best that I can
while I can.

Iman Europe 78

I say:

my steps are already indented
in the path ahead of me;
crafted perfectly and solely for my feet.
I've been given a vision that only I can see.
oh, how special I am.
how uniquely molded and favored I am.
most won't understand the plans planted in me,
but their ignorance to God's work
could never outshine the beauty in me.

Iman Europe 79

I say:

Lord,

thank you for working in me, on me, through me and around me. grant me the wisdom to decipher what is for me from what isn't, the strength to walk away from undeserving places, and the courage to walk into blessings you have reserved for me. allow me to be a blessing in return.

Amen.

Iman Europe 80

I say:

I am happy because I have chosen to be.
through flaws and disappointments. I understand
that I can't control what life gives me, but I can
choose how I will receive it. every day, I have a
choice on life's perspective, and today,
I choose to be happy.

Iman Europe 81

I say:

I am fearless.
I worry not.
I am doubtless,
I don't question my ability.
I am flawless.
I am everything I was designed to be.

Iman Europe 82

I say:

I will win because I choose to.
I will win because success has chosen me
long before I chose it.
I will win because of my resilience;
my heart made of elastic,
my skin thickened and calloused.
I will win because I know defeat.
and even when I am defeated,
I will remember that every defeat
brings me back to a win,
and I will win again.

Iman Europe 83

I say:

I appreciate myself.
I trust myself.
I accept myself.
I honor myself.
I admire myself.
I love myself.

Iman Europe 84

I say:

I am growing at God's speed.

Iman Europe 85

I say:

I am removing all attachments that do not
serve my betterment. I am creating
more space for more love.

Iman Europe 86

I say:

I am grateful for this life.
I am grateful for my health.
I am grateful for my able body.
I am grateful for my sight.
I am grateful for my ears.
I am grateful for another day to try again,
and another chance to get it right.
I am grateful for the strength
my struggle has given me,
and grateful for all of the beautiful days, too.

Iman Europe 87

I say:

I am thankful for my family.
I am thankful for my true friends.
their love is a blessing that I could never
afford. I will honor them with respect, love, and
reciprocity. I will show up for them in the
same way that they have shown up for me.

Iman Europe 88

I say:

I am being prepared for something greater
than my imagination. I have an unfathomable
blessing in my future. It will be the very thing
that changes my life for the better.
I am ready to receive it.

Iman Europe 89

I say:

I am hard-working and diligent.
I am not hindered by laziness.
I go forward with faith, fortitude and fury.
I am focused and determined.
I am committed. I will not be distracted.
I will reap the fruits of my labor.
I am aligned with my purpose.

Iman Europe 90

I say:

I am fun to be around.
my energy is magnetic.

Iman Europe 91

I say:

I am the healthiest I have ever been.

Iman Europe 92

I say:

I am free from my past.
I am trusting and trustworthy.
I am capable of giving love.
I am open to receiving love.
I am respectful. I am respectable.
I am beautiful. I am strong.
I am healed. I am prepared.
I am valuable.

Iman Europe 93

I say:

I will never stop growing.
I will never stop learning.
I will continue to evolve
and seek the highest version of myself.
complacency won't rest in me.
stagnation won't get the best of me.
there is always more to explore.

Iman Europe 94

I say:

I am not afraid—
to love, to live, to laugh, to cry,
to reflect, to forgive, to give, to try,
to release, to let go, to be alone, to grow,
to receive, to express, to be bare, to show.

I am not afraid—
of him, of her, of them, of it,
of truth, of failure, of loss, of shit.

I am not afraid of shit.
I'm bolder than I've been.
my spirit can't be broken.
fear will never win.

Iman Europe 95

I say:

my spirit is stronger than my pride.
my destiny is greater than my ego.
my faith is stronger than my fear.
my God is greater than my worry.

Iman Europe 96

i hope this book serves you during your evolution, and as you grow, i hope you return here and find new quotes that speak to where you are. the chrysalis is a place of transformation, and although the isolation is necessary, it can tend to feel lonely. i hope that this book serves as comfort in those times, and if you ever need a little light, you have a place to find it. wishing you peace and prosperity on your journey. thanks for reading.

-iman europe

p.s. be sure to tweet/post a picture of your favorite quote. i'd love to see which quote or affirmation resonated with you.

<u>**twitter:**</u> @imaneurope
<u>**instagram:**</u> @imaneurope
<u>**email:**</u> ie@imaneurope.com

Copyright © 2018

www.ingramcontent.com/pod-product-compliance
Lightning Source LLC
Chambersburg PA
CBHW060202050426
42446CB00013B/2950